We Love The Gov

Sixty Nine, Still Blind, But Doin' Fine

by Simon Mills

PUBLISHERS OF O.G. AUTHOR GENIUSES

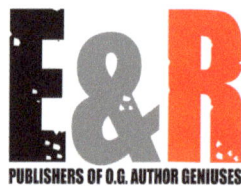

Originally published on May 20, 2016, in celebration of Governor Paterson's 62nd birthday. Rewritten to celebrate his 69th birthday May 20, 2023.

He was born rather young
To a fine Dad and Mom
His lineage that of genius and kings.
Suspiciously smart,
Right from the start,
With a brain that could solve many things.

Legally inclined
But legally blind,
Unaware of his supposed limitations.
His parents decreed
He was trouble indeed,
Destined to impact the nation.

Uninhibited by fear
He had definite ideas
About how great the great state could be.
Wisdom is timeless
And despite fits of blindness,
No one had vision like he.

Eager to play,
He left the DA
And became the youngest state Senator.
West side to the valley
Was right up his alley,
The same district run by his progenitor.

Questionable friends,
With questionable trends
Inspired gubernatorial status.
You served for some years
With cheers from your peers,
Despite the occasional fracas.

Though not all were planned,
Your achievements were grand
And you served out your term in triumph
They've come and they've gone
Some tried to stay on
But they were removed, defiant

The years indeed flew
And when you turned sixty-two,
This book was to honor your stature.
But time has marched on
Seven years have now gone
And today sixty nine has come at ya.

So now let's explore
What life's had in store
For the past seven years you've enraptured
What songs have been sung
And what has become
Of that fairytale filly you captured.

Another birthday was seen
in twenty nineteen
And you gifted yourself a fine gem
You got down on one knee
And said "Mary, Marry Me"
Putting batchelorhood two to an end

August the tenth
The very same year
On a boat, on a river, named East.
Mary was wed.
To the governor who then said
"First lady, let's drink plenty and feast."

And so it was done
These two became one
A marriage that was just meant to be
In a single fell swoop
You became a new troop
Mary, David, and of course Anthony

Opportunities abound
Business ventures are crowned
A pandemic gave rise to learn songs
You practiced guitar
In no time you came far
Then came Blind Dog Dave and The Throng

So all in all
It's been a fine haul
Sixty nine, a sensational number
We hope what's in store
Is sixty nine more
If not years, other sixty nine wonders

Ol' 55, may ever you thrive,
You're a legend
From the Hudson through Madison.
We love the Gov,
He's the Gov from above.
Bless the head Governor Paterson's hat is on.

David Alexander Paterson (born May 20, 1954) is an American po
itician. He was the 55th Governor of New York, in office from 200
to 2010. He was the first African American governor of New York
and also the second legally blind[1] governor of any U.S. state afte
Bob C. Riley, who was Acting Governor of Arkansas for 11 days i
January 1975.[2] Since leaving office, Paterson has been a radio tal
show host on station WOR in New York City, and was in 2014 ap
pointed Chairman of the New York Democratic Party by his succe
sor as governor, Andrew Cuomo.

After graduating from Hofstra Law School, Paterson worked in th
District Attorney's office of Queens County, New York, and on th
staff of Manhattan Borough President David Dinkins. In 1985, he
was elected to the New York State Senate to a seat that was once
held by his father, former New York Secretary of State Basil Paterson. In 2003, he rose to the position of Senate Minority Leader.
Paterson was selected as running mate by then-New York Attorne
General and Democratic Party gubernatorial nominee Eliot Spitze
in the 2006 New York gubernatorial election. Spitzer and Paterso
were elected in November 2006 with 69 percent of the vote, and P
terson took office as lieutenant governor on January 1, 2007.
Paterson was sworn in as governor of New York on March 17, 2008

www.ingramcontent.com/pod-product-compliance
Lightning Source LLC
Chambersburg PA
CBHW040740150426

42813CB00064B/2968